Loving After Chaos

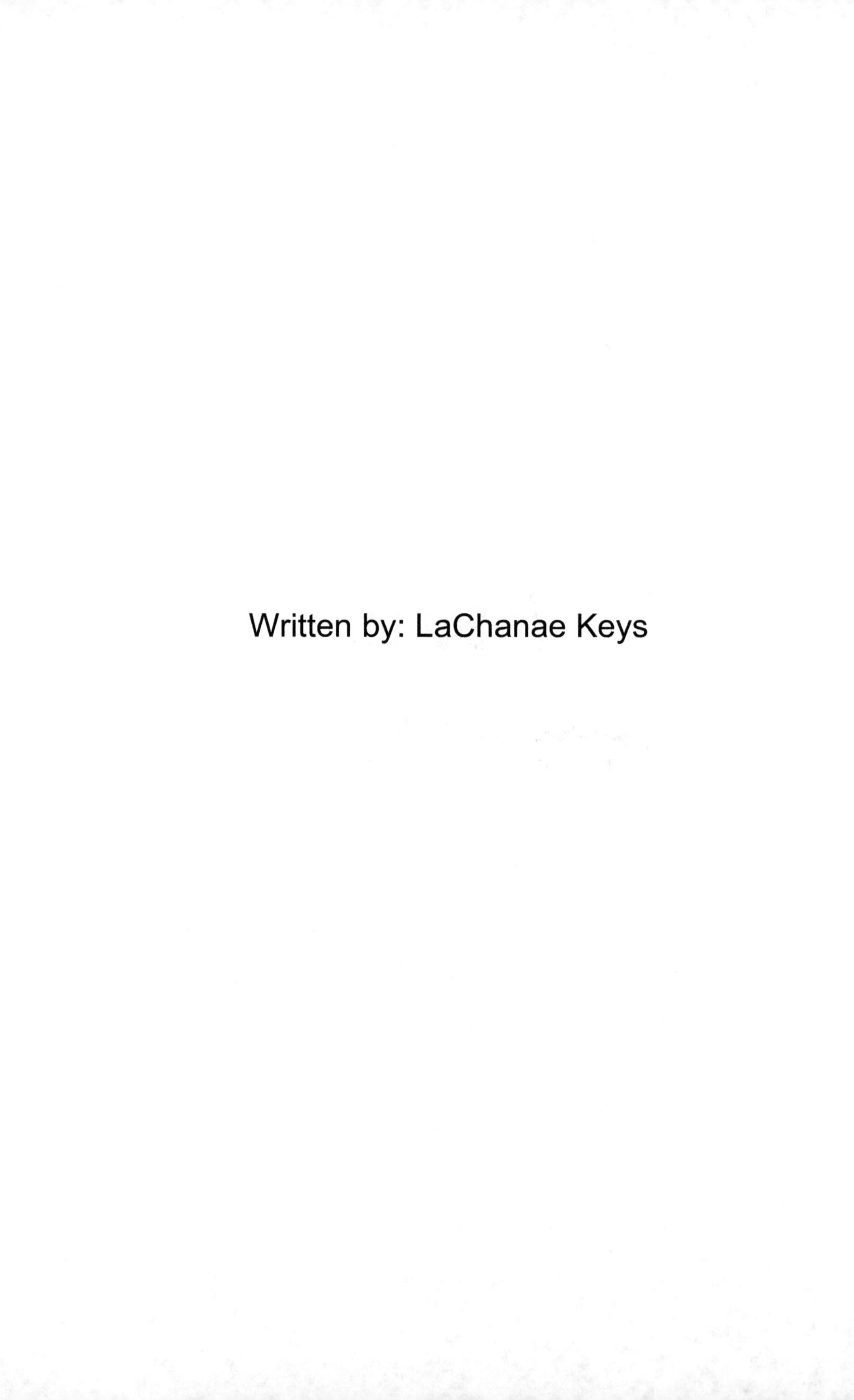

Written by: LaChanae Keys

Introduction

Hello readers, welcome back. I take it that you enjoyed the first book or you want to know what's happening. Either way thank you, I appreciate you. I know it took a while to finish this book, I just saw a lot of mistakes I made in the first book. I did say that I am dsylexic right so please don't judge me. I am not perfect, nobody walking on this earth is. As long as the message was clear that's my main thing. I also have been living my best life. It has taken some twists and turns, things happened that I cannot make up. After Ray was gone I was able to start focusing on what made me happy. I started working out, meditating daily, reading my word and focusing more on my kids. My kids saw a different side of me, "happy." Bri said, "Mommie you're silly, only kids are supposed to be silly." Little did she know this was who I was, a happy person. I just wasn't happy when Ray was around, I was always lethargic. I read that negative energy can drain your energy, it makes you lazy and not motivated to do anything. When someone else said that to Ray but in a different form he didn't take heed to it. "Marie is always tired." Ray said, "That's not good bro that means she's unhappy." A dear friend of mine, Sean said, "That's not why, she's just lazy." "No man I'm telling you I had a wife, you hear me? A wife so I knew that was the reason she was tired all the time." Sean said, I was standing there the whole time and I was like wow Ray still didn't want to hear the truth even coming from a Man with experience. I was just so happy I was free from him but I still didn't heal from him. I should have before I decided to step back out there. I had to kiss a few frogs or should I say tadpoles, to end up with my King but was it all worth it? Read and find out. Oh I would also like to add I'm not claiming to belong to any religious organizations. I definitely didn't take the righteous path on my journey to healing but it worked for me. I'm definitely not encouraging my behavior but it's my life I will not apologize for living it. Proceed with caution!

Chapter 1

Where do I begin? Leaving off where I did something hurtful, when you're hurt and not fully healed you make irrational decisions. Of course you regret them but at the end of the day, you know it shouldn't have happened anyway. Now I am really focused on trying new things, putting myself out there a little bit. Being told that no one else is going to want you consistently, takes a toll on your self-esteem. You would start to believe that no one wants you, so you're scared to actually try something with someone. That's why healing is a very important part of the self love process. After my family read my first book they asked me why I didn't reach out to them for help? Honestly I am the type of person that's going to try to figure out how to get myself out of situations, before I ask for help. I got myself in the situation in the first place. My auntie who lives in Easton PA, used to let us take a shower when we would visit her. I would tell her, "I've been riding for a long time so I would like to freshen up." I wasn't telling her the whole truth; it felt like I was lying. I definitely was not trying to tell her I was homeless. My auntie definitely was a blessing to us in our struggle, she didn't even know it. She cooked and we definitely ate. I appreciate her for that, thanks Murph.

So after I dropped Ray off to his Mother's house, I still had to deal with him. "Can I call you it's about Faith? Can I call you to talk, it's about Val from the credit union?" Ray was doing anything and everything to hear my voice, also to make sure there was no other Man around Bri. Which is something that I never did even when she was a baby. That's when they are unaware of what's going on around them. Also they can't talk, and tell the other parent what's going on. Just like I found out from my daughter that her Dad had a girlfriend. I am just not that type of parent to introduce my children to everyone I am talking to. Like I said in the last book about the car being in my name, Ray found a way to sign the title over to him, we just needed to go get the document notarized. I had to pick him up and take him to the place, even while I was doing him a favor, he still was ungrateful and we argued about something small like a wrong turn. As y'all can see I was still doing favors for him even after it was over and done, that's just the person I am. Although I said I wasn't going to give him the title because he didn't want me to leave Delaware. I remember saying; "I should be petty and say no." I still did it, after he called the police on me, after all the pain he caused me. I didn't hate Ray, I just knew I would never go back to him. In the month of May 2020 Bri and I went to South Carolina.

While we were in SC, I wasn't getting any sleep, Bri was suffering in her private area. I was really concerned because she also told me sometimes she sleeps with a boy. Bri said, "When Amiyah comes over she sleeps at the top bunk, and me and Marshall sleep at the bottom." I confronted Ray about that too, I don't know these people. Also, Marshall is older than Bri. "What's wrong?" she replied "I wiped too hard." I wasn't buying that so I kept questioning Bri until she told me, her Meema made her put a diaper on when she goes to bed. I was so irate so I texted Ray: "I know it's late but I don't want to forget, putting a diaper on Bri is not a good idea, she has a diaper rash and is crying when she pees because it burns." Ray's response was, "Can you talk?" I called him and we spoke. I expressed deeply how I felt. Ray said that Bri is not fully potty trained. That was the strangest thing to me, Bri was four at this time instead of not allowing her to drink after a certain time and make her use the bathroom before bed. They put a diaper on Bri, they definitely could've used Pull-ups that would have been better than diapers. I guess the diapers are cheaper than Pull-ups, so I told Ray if money was an issue I could pay for it. What type of people put a diaper on a toddler? I was irate because my baby was in pain and it could've been avoided.

Progressing on, I was still trying to be cordial with Ray. While I was in South Carolina I was trying to meet up with James to take my pictures for my birthday shoot. James was giving me the run around. I sent him a text "I hope all is well." "It is, how are you?" James wanted to see a picture of the dress, then a picture with me in the dress, he asked if I tried the dress on. I told him I will take a picture for him after I am done braiding my mother's hair. I was there for a week, James said he would try to get to me as soon as possible, he was just busy. I was understanding, it was the second month of Covid so people were still trying to get adjusted to living their life in fear that someone might spread it to them. It was all new, so I never saw James in the month of May. Ray and I were still communicating for the sake of Bri. I set up a skype profile for Bri so she could communicate with him. I told Ray that it feels like he wants to control my life with Bri. Ray's response was. "You're starting to worry me, don't do anything crazy. I know it's tough being alone now having to face yourself. Hence distract yourself from yourself. Praying for you shabbat shalom." Wow I was like wow I texted back, "I'm good. I'm really tired of being put down by you and your family and after all that I have done. My love can be seen and accepted elsewhere and it's just not in Delaware." Ray sent a long message so to sum it up he was trying to say he can't help me with my feelings because it was no longer his place. All he was only able to help me with is the coparenting aspect. Ray still didn't understand how I felt, and I just no longer had the energy to show him, it was far too late. I ended the conversation with, "I appreciate you and I am here if you need me (my weakness)." All I really wanted was to tell him was. "I just need you and your family to respect me. I was raised to handle my business. I moved out of my parents house, when I was 17 years old after I graduated High School. I am capable of keeping a roof over my children's head and keeping their bellies well fed." I definitely didn't want a relationship with Ray. It was over for me when I dropped him off at his Mother's house.

When Bri and I returned from South Carolina something transpired between Ray and I. We were arguing and we started discussing going to court. Ray threw in my face that his mother is a case worker so I would lose. I know that the last thing I said was, "I am not trying to go to court." I felt like we could be civilized adults and we could work out some type of arrangements. I also suggested we put something in writing and get it notarized. Thinking back on it now I am glad that we didn't, you'll see why.

Chapter 2

"Imy bby" Leon texted "I miss you too." "We have to link up very soon." "Alright, I will be going down South next week and I was going to ask if you wanted to go to Vegas?" "I'm going to Vegas this weekend, you should just go when I go." Leon suggested, "I have to work so I will see what I can do and I will let you know." I did make arrangements to make it out there, I left right after work but before I left I texted him my boarding pass. I asked Leon, "Are we going to go rounds like old times?" "Yes lord Asap" "Ok baby." Alright so I got to Vegas, I rented a car, then I called my cousin Lisa so that I could go to her house. When I arrived I saw how my cousin was living and I was so proud of her.

Lisa is living on her own with her three kids, she has a car, and she is taking care of her kids. That made me happy to see that she can do it, and with three kids, so I was going to be alright with my two. I always felt the need to have someone around, so it was giving me a sense of clarity, I can do this by myself. I let Leon know I was there, he was at some Casino gambling I was watching a basketball game, I forgot who was playing. I was just trying to stay in and safe because COVID-19 was out there, so I was in the room waiting for him to arrive. I had to meet Leon in the lobby to let him up to my room, you can only enter with a key card. As I am walking Leon was walking behind me, I am getting a lot of stares from guys and I see it. Head turns, guys tapping their friends to look at me. I felt like a lil celebrity or whatever. I am sure Leon saw it too, when we got off the elevator it was less crowded. Leon hugged me from the back and said, "Damn baby." Before we got to the room Leon wanted me to take a picture of him. I did, then we went to the room, I had my laptop out Leon asked, "What's this for your fans only?" I laughed and said, "No." "I got one you want to be on it?" "Alright as long as my face isn't in it." Leon said "I don't have a fans only." "I know." I knew he wasn't serious so I was playing along to see how far he would go and to find out if he really had one. We were intimate and then he said, "Baby don't let me fall asleep." Leon fell asleep so did I for a little while he woke up, gave me a long hug and left.

The next day I decided to drive to surprise my Grandmother with flowers. I was in the store, the line was so long and I only had flowers. This lady started chatting with me. The lady was with her daughter. I told her how I was surprising my Grandmother with flowers. The lady said to her daughter, "Aww look she's surprising her Grandmother with flowers." There was a check out register in the bakery section so she said, "Come check out with us and use our rewards card for a discount." I didn't know who those women were, but I thank them because that line was ridiculous. I arrived at my Grandmother's house. My Aunt Sally opened the door and she embraced me with a warm hug. Then I saw my Grandmother, she was smiling hard with her high cheekbones. We hugged, I gave her the flowers. My Grandmother said, "Sarah said one of Jenny's kids was in Vegas but I didn't know which one." She was so happy to see me she started to call my Cousins and I spoke to most of them. I missed my Grandmother's 80th birthday party, so I had to do something to make up for it. When you miss out on life and family trying to please someone, that's not the one for you, instead you should be enjoying life together. With that being said I told my Grandmother and my Aunt everything that I was going through. I told her why I missed her 80th birthday. I tried not to cry because family is everything to me. And to not be there for a huge milestone in my Grandmother's life, the one who helped raise me didn't sit well with me. I needed that, I felt better after I told them, I definitely didn't want them finding out from my book. My Aunt Sally said, "We all go through it, and when we get out we are like, what the hell was I thinking." I agreed with her one hundred percent, I didn't know why I stayed so long. Ray was always promising change and I held on to hope thinking things will get better. It was also the fear of starting over no one wants to do that when you feel like things are supposed to work out. You have all the hope in the world that the person you fell in love with is still in there somewhere. Also it's the adrenaline you feel when you are in that Toxic relationship is addictive.

When I left Vegas and returned to Delaware I had a new sense of being. My confidence was coming back slowly but surely. The attention that I was receiving from the people in Vegas was lit. I am finally free to do as I please after my trip to Vegas I was feeling like myself again. Leon and I would text we were supposed to meet up again but work consumed my time. Everytime I get back from a trip, Ray starts an argument with me. This time it was about me not letting him know when I was getting back, which had to be sooner than I expected because I had to return to work. Ray texted a long message saying; *"It's not fair to my family that you didn't let us know you were coming back. They do have to get her stuff ready."* It wasn't a big deal to me, I could wash her clothes. I told him I was on the plane with no service. Ray still wanted to know my every move. Bri was with him so I decided to wait to pick her up because I was off the next day, but I had to work the day after. I told him Bri should just stay there until I had more days off. I was just confused why he was arguing with me and Bri was with him, she was safe, my location had nothing to do with him. Ray was always complaining about not having enough time with her, now he has too much time and then he still complains I didn't get it. Ray said his family had to work, when his mom didn't even have a job. Ray was just trying to give me a hard time along with a headache. It was definitely working.

Chapter 3

I went to visit my parents in South Carolina, I reconnected with Donald, we texted and spoke on the phone a few times before we met up. Donald spent the night with me and he had me laughing at his jokes all night. We spoke about the past and how I was uncomfortable. Donald was the guy I tried to be intimate with, while Ray and I were still living together in South Carolina. I was with one man faithfully, most people don't know what that is nowadays. It was awkward for me to just become intimate with someone, who just re-entered my life, when I had all these memories in my head of the past. That was because I was still around my past while trying to get over my past. That was impossible, you can't heal in an unhealthy environment, no matter how hard you try. Although I was mentally done with Ray back then, physically it took some time for me to get used to someone else. Especially when all you hear in your head is; *"Guys just want what's between your legs, they don't care about you."* That can ruin anything for you even if your body wants to, your mind can stop you from enjoying it. That's what happened to me in the past with Donald.

When I left to go back to Delaware I texted Donald flirting with him telling him how I felt. I remember in the past I would just stop talking to him, so I wasn't trying to do that again. Donald's response to me flirting with him was; "Stop it you're being extra." So y'all know what I did I stopped talking to him, he said I wasn't in close proximity anyway. I just know I wasn't tolerating bs at this point, from no one. I wasn't in close proximity so it was understandable, but I was in SC every month. I was home sick and also I believe I was trying to recreate what Ant and I had with someone else. That was really impossible, what Ant and I shared was special to me. Although we were miles apart he was the closest Man to my heart. Although he lied to me too, but hey that's life. It was something I needed to go through to make me stronger and wiser when it came to Men.

That fling was over as soon as it started. Two months went by, I am planning to return to SC again so I got in contact with James, I still wanted him to take my pictures. James and I are texting while I am hanging out with my sisters, we were drinking White Zinfandel. "Save me some." James said, "I will try, you know we're not hanging out." "Why not?" "Because James you're playing games." "I'm not I want you to come over, I'm staying with family right now so I have to wait until they sleep out of respect." I respected that so I said, "I will get a room so we can fully enjoy each other's company without worrying about being too loud, laughing and talking etc. I will pick you up." "Lol I have a car you don't have to pick me up. Where is your room?" "I'm about to get one, I'll text you the info." "Oh dang you don't have it yet, what side of town?" I sent the address James replied, "Not too far at all. Are you already there?" "I'm driving now." "Ok just tell me when you get there and shower and all that." "Ok, here about to shower." I showered, I also had to use the bathroom because I was so nervous. I haven't been alone with him in a while. I told him about how my confidence was low because Ray made me feel like crap all those years. Ray put me in a mental prison, he was very repetitive, Ray got that from his mother. April would repeat everything more than twice to get her point across, or she's trying to convince you that what is being said is right. Ray would do the same thing, beat it into your head until you start to believe it.

With that being said I didn't know how to make myself presentable to someone without feeling a little insecure. James remembered things about me although he never experienced being with me that made me smile. James arrived and surprisingly I wasn't as shy as I thought I would be, I felt comfortable with him. We talked for a while about why we never had the opportunity back then because I wasn't fully over Ray and I was trying to save my family. While Ray and I split, I met James and we were never intimate. I was being loyal to Ray so I never replied to James's message until two years later. True definition of loyalty it didn't matter that James looked way way way way way way way better than Ray I was LOYAL. After we talked James said, "Ok time to get nasty." I agreed but I was still a little nervous. James got on his knees like he was about to say his prayers but he didn't. Oh wow it was amazing and I don't let that happen to me often but he knows what to do. We were at it all night but we would take breaks and talk in between. I knew he had to work the next morning so I wasn't trying to keep him up all night but I was really enjoying myself. I was able to be myself with him. "I was just focused on pleasing you." James said, "Well you did an awesome job." James left around 3 a.m. I texted him saying, "I hope you made it home safely." "Yea I didn't wyd?" I was concerned, "Why are you ok? I'm laying down." James didn't reply but I'm guessing he's ok. I sent him a message explaining how he made me feel last night and I wanted to see him again soon. I wasn't able to, I had to head back to Delaware.

I didn't want to leave, James and I texted from time to time. James would ask me what I was eating and cooking, he would say yuck or nasty just playing though, he made me laugh and smile. Sometimes we would go days without texting which was alright with me we were not obligated to speak daily. When I return to Delaware I am still dealing with Ray and trying to work at the same time. Whenever I get back Ray gets so mad because he knows, when I am down there I am with somebody. I knew a lot of people there from meeting them while working at the hospital, social media and other places. When I arrived back in town I told Ray I would be there at 6 pm. I texted him, "I don't know about bringing Bri tonight I'm tired." Ray agreed to meet at 9 a.m I asked,"Where?" he replied, "Your job." I really didn't want to meet there but hey I didn't want to argue. Ray told me to not pack her bag because he had enough clothes for her stay,

When Ray arrived he was late as usual, good thing I told him 9 a.m but I had to go in at 9:30 a.m. Ray definitely had a motive to why he wanted to come to my job. Ray caused a scene with no audience because I parked out the way. Ray was shouting out, "Coke head!" Ray said that I am a liar because his mother drove by my house and saw my car in the driveway. I told him, I was almost in town, it could have been 30 minutes 5 minutes I do know I wasn't home yet. What really made me mad was if they really wanted to get her, they could've picked her up, while they were stalking me. This family just wanted to make my life a living hell, they were doing such a great job. I went to work mad, everyone knew what I was dealing with although I tried to keep people out of my business. Ray made me so irate I couldn't control my feelings. I really didn't care anymore, I used to always go to work and pretend everything was alright. This time I didn't care because I knew I wasn't going back to him. Ray was trying to get me fired from my job, it didn't work but the fact that he did that was childish. I would never try to ruin his means of living, I couldn't even look at him the same. Ray was a real life coward in my eyes. Mad because he knew I was done so if I got fired I would have to depend on him to help me pay my rent. Ray thought that would open the door for him to come back. Sike, he tried and I really didn't care if anyone heard either because I would've been willing to take a drug test. I wasn't doing any drugs, I was high off life, I felt like I wasn't living when I was with Ray. Everyday was a test, a drill, and a headache, I was over it. Ray's own insecurities made him miss out on the good woman I am. Ray knew that he just didn't know how to treat me. Ray said, "I don't want to let you go because I feel like all of my work I did to help groom you. Someone else is going to benefit from it." I didn't totally disagree with his statement, Ray taught me small things about running a household as far as submitting, actually being a woman. I learned how to make African cuisines, I just didn't feel happy while doing it because he didn't appreciate me. Now that I am away I know he didn't.

Chapter 4

In the month of August Markita, my dear friend that helped me get to work and get my car repaired. Her daughter was having a birthday party before we were leaving to go to SC. We stayed so that Bri could attend her party although I was already ready to go. The girls had a good time, that's all that mattered to me. Markita was always looking out for me, she knew someone who was selling a washer and dryer for 300 dollars. At the time I didn't have it, I had to pay for more work to be done on my car. I appreciated that so here I am planning another trip to Sc. My sister Tasha was living with me at the time so we had received bad news. One of my dear friends/sister wasn't doing too well, we were trying to make it out there before it was too late but the way our work schedules were set up we didn't have the same days off so we waited.

It was too late, we were just sad reminiscing about all the good times we had with her. Laughter and tears my sister was gone the last time we spoke was when she was in Florida and she was planning to move back to SC. I was so sad I felt like people close to me didn't show any remorse or sympathy towards me or the situation. I felt alone around people that called me friend.

Moving on, check this out, I am not a narcissist but when I looked at James's page, he would say things that would correlate to what we spoke about or what I am going through. I am just going to start with the very first one I thought pertained to me. Even if it didn't it helped me get through. *"Nothing is a coincidence. Everything you're experiencing is meant to happen exactly how it's happening. Embrace the lessons. Be grateful."* I felt that because I told him I regret not spending more time with him when I had the chance. I also wasted time with Ray when I could've seen where we could've gone. *"Whatever is worrying you right now, forget about it. Take a deep breath, stay positive and know that things will get better."* I definitely was wondering how I was going to escape Delaware. *"You're tired. You're stressed. You're mentally and Physically drained. You feel alone. Struggling with the present, uncertain of the future. Like sucks right now You'll be fine I promise.. It gets better, Just keep moving forward."* I felt that because all of the above was true. I wanted to move, I just didn't know how and when. I was alone with my kids, I had no family, no one to help. *"There are moments when trouble enters our lives and we can do nothing to avoid them. But they are there for a reason. Only when we have overcome them will we understand why they were there."* More facts: I didn't know why I went through what I went through with Ray until I overcame my feelings for him. It led me to write these books so that I may help someone else get through. *"Think big and don't listen to people who tell you it can be done. Life is too short to think small."* Yes, that's why I wrote my book inspiration at its fullest. *"You are beautiful, never forget that. In a world of 7.1 billion people, there is only one you. So take care of you because the world needs you."* I Felt that so I had to start checking myself before I left the house so I could be appealing, not for anyone else but myself. I also explained to him that I was trying to gain my confidence back because it was stripped away from me. *"Be so busy loving your life that you have no time for hate, regret or fear."* I told him I was afraid to share my story but I did. *"The best way to gain self confidence is to do what you are afraid to do."* Yes I told him I was scared to start broadcasting I am shy which is true and it shows in my videos I don't think I have a video personality. *"Don't be in such a rush to figure everything out. Embrace the unknown and let your life surprise you."* Yes because we would go days without communicating and I would wonder why. *"The truth is, unless you let go, unless you forgive yourself, unless you forgive the situation, unless you realize that the situation is over you cannot move forward."* I definitely should have replied to this, "Umm sir I did all of that already I'm ready to move forward." *"Life changes for the better when you take action instead of making excuses."* This is true I was procrastinating when it came to writing. *"Be patient, good things will come."* I had no choice but to be patient. *"If you truly want to be respected by the ones you love, you must prove to them that you can survive without them." "If you don't love yourself you'll always be chasing after people who don't love you either." "In case no one told you today, you are needed, you are stronger than you think you are, you are doing great, you are here for a reason, don't give up."* I think I am almost done, this was like a daily thing for him. Around the time my sister died he posted this *"If you're having a down day have it. Let yourself feel emotions but don't stay there."*

That touched my heart. I never confronted him about these posts while he was posting them because I didn't want to seem egotistical nor did I want him to stop posting. *"The one who is meant for you encourages you to be your best, but still loves and accepts you at your worst."* Yes when we first reconnected I felt like I was looking rough and I told him. I look rough right now I know. *"The path of the future is uncertain and blurred. The walk is long and tiring. But in the end you will realize it was all worth it."* Definitely felt this, I know we go through things only to make us stronger. *"When one door closes, another opens; but we often look so long and so regretfully upon the closed door that we do not see the one which has opened for us."* I understood that but once I closed that door it never reopened never ever ever. *"The more you know who you are and what you want the less you let things upset you."* I believe that's because I would never sweat him about not responding, I would let him know he sucks at communicating. I texted him in August to let him know I will be there in September and I would love to see him. James asked why I was coming and I told him just to visit. Another quote before I arrived *"Don't ask yourself what the world needs, ask yourself what makes you come alive. And then go and do that. Because what the world needs is people who have come alive."* Ya'll what really got me was this video he made a day before I went to SC and he said, "Just because", it was so sexy. The same day he came to my room before he got there he posted. *"The greatest danger for most of us is not that our aim is too high and we miss it but that it is too low and we reach it."* *"Life is not about finding yourself. Life is about creating yourself."* Alright so when I got to Columbia first thing first I have to see my babies they lost their mother my sister I loved her life. Bones was the life of the party and I missed her already.

When we got to the house to see her girls I cried as soon as I saw the middle child who looks just like Bones all grown up. I said, "I'm sorry for crying." she said,"You're ok." It has been years since I've seen them. The girls were alright hanging in there. I'm sure some days were hard for them, I know because it was hard for me. I would cry out of the blue thinking about her not being here and how we were supposed to spend time together. My sister Tasha and I saw a butterfly on the porch and it would fly away then come right back and sit by the door. I started crying more and took a picture of the butterfly and I said, "That was her, she wasn't ready to leave, she wanted to make sure her girls were alright." I was so emotional that losing her showed me that life is too short for you to be wasting your time, if you're with someone who keeps you away from your family and friends then LEAVE!!!!! It is so unhealthy, you don't want to be living with regret wishing you can go back in time. While I was going through all of that Markita my dear friend called, "You know you're supposed to be at work." No, hey how are you? Is everything alright? I responded saying, "The managers knew that I was not coming in." She said, "Alright." We got off the phone. I had to focus on my Daughter's birthday party. I was running around getting things, I texted James my room address he texted back saying, "I didn't even know you were here." I was laughing because he did know because I told him days before I arrived, so I just said, "Well you do now." "What did you do all day?" I replied, "Shopped for a party. U?" "What you getting?" James disregarded my U? "I got a few decorations etc . What are you up to?" "Just got off. When's the party?" "Whenever you're ready." He replied, "Smh" "Why lol?" I asked, "I'm trying to be considerate, Oh lol My mind is in the gutter tomorrow." I was so embarrassed he was literally talking about the birthday party and I was just thinking about us. James asked where we were having it? I told him he also wanted to know what the outfit looked like, I really don't know why and I didn't ask. I asked James, "What are you doing after nine?" he said, "Not sure, wbu?" I told him I was picking my sis up from work then we are going to take shots. "Where y'all drinking at?" "My sister Tasha's boyfriend's house." "O dang that sucks I want some." "Why? you can come lol." "Yea yea we will see lol." " For real I didn't even open the bottle, see I'm nice." I texted James, "Headed to my room now." "Why are you heading there so early?" "Idk do you want to go somewhere?" "Nah you good. Where are you at?" "I just dropped my sister off to her bf on Forest Drive." "Got you, I thought you were back at the hotel." "I'm 10 mins away, I was on my way but my sis had to stop at the store first." " It's cool I was just messing with you." "You are soooooooooo not funny lol." I said, "I know but tell me when you get there and all clean and stuff." "Ok", I texted him when I got out of the shower. "I'm clean and stuff. Lol" James texted back, "Clean and stuff with the emoji with the hand on the head." I just laughed and he texted and told me he was about to be on his way. I said, "Ok" James asked for the room number? I gave it to him before he arrived, there was a bug in the room, I put the trash can over it. When James arrived he had a hard time finding the room. I had to go outside to retrieve him from the parking lot. He greeted me with a hug and said, "You're trying to get me shot." I said, "No I'm not, why do you say that?" James said, "You got me out here." I just laughed when we got to the room, I had asked him to do me a favor and he said, "No it's late." I begged, "Please please please please." "What is it?" "Can you get that bug from under the trash can? I didn't want to kill it so I just captured it, do you think it's still alive?" James asked, "Do you want to see?" I squealed "No!" When he got back I said, "I wonder if when the air hit then he came back to life." James said, "Nah it's over for him." James and I were talking just vibing, I told him how I believed in Ray before he believed in himself. I bought him a laptop so that he can finish out his dream. I also told him how I wanted to move but I didn't know how, the last time I tried to leave Ray crashed my car. I am just trying to avoid things like that happening. James said I should've never gotten him a laptop because a man that wants something done is going to make sure he has the necessary tools to become successful. James also said, "If you want to leave this time you know you will not be able to tell him, you are just going to have to do it." We were talking about relationships and he said he's been single for six years. I asked why his response was, "Because I go too hard in a relationship." I asked, "Isn't that what you're supposed to do?" James started comparing other people's relationships and how they have problems. I told him every relationship has problems, it's just how you overcome them together. James also asked, how many times do I get approached when I go out? I answered, "That doesn't matter if I could be loyal to a man that treated me like crap for years, imagine how loyal I could be to someone who actually treats me right." I was trying to get him to see that, I thought that since I didn't reply to his message it was enough proof that I am a loyal woman.

James looks 100000000000000000000000 times better than Ray so who wouldn't reply to him. After our talk we were intimate, James started kissing my lips below. Round one began for us then. We talked for awhile then he went back down on me, I was crying he wined and dined me Lil Wayne style. I told him, "You almost made me say I love you." I had to eat my words literally. When we started the next round it slipped out, I was hoping he didn't hear me so I tried to cover it up and say, "I love it." Oh well he knew what he was doing to me. I was floating on cloud 9, I didn't ever want to come down. I told him to let me know when he makes it home, he did. I had to get ready to head back myself. Tasha and I were on the road back to Delaware. A day later he texted, "How are you?" "I'm ok, how are you?" "Same just chilling wyd?" I didn't want to appear clingy so I didn't respond, I just texted him the next day. "Gm handsome, have a great day." He texted, "Good morning, how are you?" I replied "I'm ok a bit sore, I will be better when I get off. How are you?" "I am great, just at work. What you sore for?" "Ok that's awesome.. Sore from… You." "Not my fault." "You're right." We texted on and off for a month. James birthday came around and I remember when we were together, he saw my candle melt. James asked me where I got it from and if he could have mine I said, "No go to Walmart." James said, "I don't be in Walmart long enough to find stuff like that." So Since I had the address to his house I bought him a candle melt and sent it to his house with a birthday card. "Smh I appreciate the gift Thank you. Got me by surprise." "You're welcome." " I really appreciate it I was scared to open it because I knew for a fact I didn't order anything." "I am all about the element of surprise and besides that's just a little something. I'm happy that you appreciate it." I decided to send him that gift because I knew I wouldn't see him for his birthday.

Chapter 5

Meanwhile I am trying to get adjusted with work and losing someone close to me that I haven't seen in years. I was supposed to go to her house for her birthday, I never made it because I was with Ray. So if he wasn't going I couldn't go either, he always thought that when I stepped out I was seeing another man. It was just his own guilty conscious eating away at himself. If he couldn't trust me when he was around then he obviously wasn't doing something right. If he had the confidence to know that when I'm not with him I was still with him. Ray was afraid that I would meet someone that would treat me better than he was. If he wasn't worried about that then he wouldn't have to worry about me looking twice at someone. When I returned to work I brought Marikta's daughter a gift bag from Bri's birthday party. I got Markita a key chain and shot glass souvenirs. She tells me to go in my car for a second I guess while she talks on the phone. I listened, she probably had some business to take care of over the phone. We are on ok terms I didn't tell her about James because her sex life was dry so I didn't want her feeling some type of way. One day I got in her car only to see the key chain on the floor, I felt some type of way. I let a few days go by to see if she got my Daughter something for her birthday and she never did. This is me, you can treat me any type of way and I'll ignore it for a while, but my children. I don't play about them, not that my Daughter was looking forward to a gift, it was just the principle. I got her something for her birthday, her Daughter a birthday gift and also her Goddaughter birthday. I at least expected her to get a gift for my Daughter. Markita's Daughter wasn't at the party but she got a gift bag. This is possibly what really put the icing on the cake for me I received a text message saying; "You and your boy just didn't give a what yesterday." I read the message like wtf I don't like the way that sounds. I called Markita, "Hey what's up?" "So yall didn't work yesterday?" I was confused so I asked her to elaborate and she said, "You only made one pan of pasta. Also the meat wasn't prepped." "I prepared enough at least for them to get started, if they run out of food then it's simple to make the pasta. So is that all ma'am you enjoy the rest of your day goodbye." Click!! I hung up the phone, I was like that mess had me hot. You come to me on my day off about something I couldn't do anything about. You're at work so you can make what they need. I couldn't help that my food was good but I know I made enough and possibly night shift used day shift food.

Either way don't come at me like that, like I just came to work and did nothing. I took it to facebook and I posted "Most of you were never my friends, I was just yours. I know the difference Now." That was facts so me being me, I can't be fake it's not in my D.N.A. so when I was at work I ignored her. I went on break by myself and sat in my car, then she came to me while we were in the kitchen of the hospital and asked, "Did I do something to you?" I replied "No." Which was true she didn't, I just saw her for who she really was. Another day she said, "I know you're going through something so I am going to give you time to yourself." I snickered like you don't know the half. Another day she asked, "Are we good?" I answered, "Yeah." I started coming in not saying anything to her but talking to everyone else, especially the people she didn't like. Markita came up to me for the last time and asked, "Is this how things are going to be?" I replied, "Yeah I guess so." Then one day I walked in on her talking about me rolling with the snakes so I was like, "Yep all day everyday." Then she changed the subject because I decided to sit in the office for a while and check my email. The same person she was on the phone with was the same girl I knew everything about before I even met her. When I met her I already had the persona of who I thought she was. Also her other girlfriend I knew all about, before I met her so I had to reevaluate the situation and I saw that unfriending her wasn't a bad idea. I am pretty sure that if she was telling their business to me and she just met me. What makes me think my secrets are safe with her, nah no thank you I don't want any parts of that. I would literally work around her and not say a word, once I see you for who you are I am not going to be fake about it. I used to do this girl's hair for free and not once did she offer to pay. I only did it the first two times because she was looking out for me when I didn't have my car. Marikita would wake up in the morning so that I could go to work. I felt like that was the least I could do, but at least offer to pay or pay half price. One day she called and asked me to do something, I said I can't do it because I was doing someone's hair and I am getting paid for it. Yea I was being petty but she got the message because she got her hair done elsewhere. Fool me once, shame on you, fool me twice can't put the blame on you. I was nobody's fool, I recognized that early on so I knew how to play her. People at work started asking me, "You don't talk to Markita?" I explained what happened and how I felt. I wasn't in the wrong about how I was feeling, nor how I was going about things. I know she was scared that I wasn't her friend because I knew a lot about her that she didn't want other people knowing. Little did she know I was far from the person she was, her secrets were safe with me, I am not that type of person to throw anyone under the bus even on bad terms. That's just not me, that takes too much of your energy.

Back to my love life the last time I was in SC James played Pop smoke song Mood swings on his story after he saw me. Also he was still posting things. I was paying attention but it was like he was playing games. James would hint at how he felt on facebook. Or drop hints for me to show up to his job which is just strange, I only came to his job in the past by accident. I didn't know he worked there. I was just looking for a job. James and I would text every now and then I told him I was coming out there. Then he said he had some things to do, so I pushed the days back so I could see him. I also decided to work that weekend for someone. Other things I was dealing with, Ray was still texting me almost everyday he asked if my son wanted water Ice trying hard to slide back in my life no thanks. I texted him about Bri continuing her education on ABC mouse. I also texted him letting him know that in November I will be going to Vegas the 12th-16th. I asked if he wanted to keep Bri or if she could stay with my parents since I had to pick my sisters up. I also told him I will be in South Carolina next month. Ray agreed on watching her while I went out of town. Ray and I are communicating about Bri and her education, things are going pretty well.

In the month of October a guy named Shawn from my past got in contact with me. Shawn and I were good friends in the past, we would shoot hoops. We would play all around the world and we would just hang out from time to time. One day we were intimate, it wasn't all that pleasurable for me but he remembers fireworks. I felt like that ruined our friendship. Moving on years later he came back, "How have you been? How are the kids?" "I'm great, the kids are good, what about yourself? what's new?" "Just got hired. Finally, I can't wait to start. Trying to purchase a house by next year. Other than that, just the same old Shawn." "That's great congratulations." Shawn then asked, "When is the next time you will be out here?" "I will be there around the 23rd of this month." "Are we getting up?old times?" I told him I will let him know when I get in town. I was feeling Shawn, I know y'all are thinking like what about James. Well this is what happened, I was getting more attention and vibes from Shawn so he was my first priority when I got to SC. I was always working so he said I deserve a trophy, I really didn't have too many days off. When I did I tried to make the best of it by not being in the state I had nothing but bad memories in. Shawn and I would text daily and our message count started to catch up to James and I texts. That said a lot because James and I were talking way before I started talking to Shawn. Shawn would send me pictures out of the blue, I loved it. Tasha's boyfriend came and stayed the night because they attended a wedding in New Jersey. I was talking to him about the guys in SC, and he knew Shawn so I told him your boy said, "What up?" Shawn was confused so I told him his name. Shawn asked, "How did I come up?" I replied, "We were just having a general conversation." Which were just having a conversation about the guys out in Delaware versus the guys in

SC. Then James and Shawn came up and he just so happens to know him. The days are approaching for my departure to SC. When I arrive there I post that I am at Lizard Thicket. Then I received a phone call from Shawn, I told him I was dropping my sister off at home then I will be on my way to him. Shawn was ready, so was I this time. When I arrived I thought I would be nervous but I wasn't, we actually had a good time. I was loving the way he made me feel, you know how you get those butterflies in your stomach when you recall a moment that had your mind blown. Shawn asked me to text him when I arrived home. Shawn asked, "Was it everything?" I said "Yes, thanks."

When I got to my room I was preparing to leave to go to my friend's Twana house but my car wouldn't start. Me Me Me trying to be a playa, I was still texting James he had a late night working we were texting for awhile I thought he was going to come to my room. James was tired, he asked "When did you get here?" I answered, "Thursday but I only got the room for tonight. I stayed with my parents." The next day James texted, "Oh dang why didn't you call me?" I told him I was scared. I told James about my car breaking down so he seemed concerned and asked if I got it fixed. Which I did, my sister had a friend who worked on cars and he fixed it right in the parking lot. I also invited Shawn to my room but I was waiting for James to respond first. Since I texted Shawn late he never came either, so I was just there in a room with me and my thoughts. I felt so all alone but it was what I needed. I cried myself to sleep because I was trying to fill a void with pleasure but at the end of the day I felt so all alone. Yes I had two men in my life that wanted me physically but that wasn't enough. Oh yes I reconnected with Twana, that's my girl I told her about everything and what I went through with Ray. She said she already knew he was that type of person because that was how her ex-husband was. Twana was happy that I finally left him. When I was back in

Delaware I texted James a song Faded to Sade by Lyrica ft. Chris Brown and I said, "You have a lot of making up to do." "Hi, how are you, how much?" "I told him I'm a little sexually frustrated but I will live. How are you? Two days worth." "Oh nah. That's not good. I am great just about to shower. How's your car?" "Yea I will be ok,I have been without for more than 125 days. My car is up and running, I made it back to this place. Thanks for asking." "Oh dang that's crazy, you got it fixed in Columbia?" "Yes it was hard but I am picky, I don't just give myself to multiple and random guys. Yes right in the hotel parking lot. My sister's friend fixed it. Side Note: no skating invite, I know how to skate a little bit lol." I also insisted that it might have been a date. James responded, "I feel you on the random people. I just be to myself, but glad you got the car fixed. I went out to get a good cardio exercise in. I didn't invite anyone. I am very much a solo person when I go out." "True same I am finally happy again. Yes it was the starter. It took him like 30 minutes to change it. Ok that's nice and understandable." I was happy again, I knew that since I started going out by myself. You know you love yourself when you can go places by yourself, spoil yourself, cater to yourself. I started treating myself how I wanted to be treated by someone else.

Shawn and I were still communicating with each other he would call sometimes out of the blue. Like he knew I wasn't with anyone I liked, it showed confidence. Like I know when I call her she will pick up unless she is doing something because he knew it wasn't with anyone else. Well at least no one in Delaware. My birthday rolls around and James texts me, "Hello there, Happy birthday." "Hey thanks luv." "You're welcome, how are you?" "I'm blessed how are you?" "What do you have planned?" "Nothing really until the 12th, I'm going to Vegas." "How long are you going to be there?" "Until the 16th. Are you coming?" "Shoot not with all these crazy people." "Lol it's not that bad." It would've been nice for him to come have fun with me. I love when we got together it's like we are friends but we like each other. Our vibe is irreplaceable I tried to replace it but it wasn't worth it. Yes Shawn was doing things I liked but he wasn't on the same playing field as James. I texted James a picture of the Pocono's and said "We should go here." His response was "I will go out of town soon. You going to Vegas?" "Yes viva Las Vegas." "Don't spend all your money out there." "Yes Daddy!! Lol I definitely won't and don't gamble. So I'm really good just seeing family and friends." "That's good when you come back?" "On the 17th Why do you want to see me?" James didn't reply. I tried to see him before I left to go to Vegas but he was busy. James texted me right before I left to go to Vegas, "Hi just working What are you up to?" Now this is where things started going South, I can see it now. I didn't text him until I returned to Delaware which was a week later. I really don't like being ignored, just let me know you'll be busy and you won't have time. I am always communicating with him ahead of time when I want to see him, so he can tell me if he has plans or not.

Another thing I was dealing with was my sisters were literally turning against me causing a whole embarrassing scene at the airport. I decided to get a rental car and my own separate room. The things that were said to me are too hurtful to repeat and also I forgave them for it. I have just been through a lot already and I am always helping and not getting anything in return but people talking about me behind my back. I know that I do say what's on my mind and if people are offended by it then they need to re-evaluate themselves and do better. *If you can't be corrected without being offended you will never grow in life."* That's real. It's just a lot of people guilty conscious half the time that gets the best of them. If you know it's not relevant to you then you shouldn't get offended. Moving on we are still out there for family, when my brother gets there he makes us talk and hug. My brother said life is too short for us to be mad at each other, given the field he is in he said he sees it all. We agreed and forgave each other, so we are having fun eating out and drinking Fat Tuesdays. We went bowling, it was fun just hanging out with family. One morning I went to the room with my brother and cousins, they had me laughing so hard my cousin Keith said, "One day Uncle Jay was whooping Jay jr and all you hear is him whipping him like he had a *whip whip whip*." Keith said, "Uncle Jay said, say your name, then Jay Jr. said "Kunta Kinte." Keith said, "I was scared so I hid." Then Jay said, "Yea and you know why they couldn't find him because he was hidden in a little shot glass." That was funny because Keith was short growing up, they had me laughing so hard that my voice was gone. We were having so much fun.

One night I was a little too tipsy, I lost my phone at the casino, I went to security, I was so happy that someone turned it in. I was being approached by Men but I was turning them down. There was this one guy who put his number in my phone. I totally forgot I had James and I, picture as a wallpaper, bummer oh well. I had that wallpaper just for Ray so he could see who I was dealing with, a whole sexy man. I wasn't looking for a quick link anyways my womanhood decided to take its course. While my voice is going away I am also getting sleepy from the tea my cousin made for me. Then we had a discussion about the bible no matter what state we were in, the word was still in us. It was interesting until Tasha tried to fight me because she called me stupid when she didn't even know what the conversation was about. I got mad but I didn't want to fight, so I walked in the other room, my bro came and talked to me. "You know you wouldn't get mad if I called you stupid but since y'all are already not on cool terms you got offended when she said that." He was right of course he knew I never let words get to me, I was never that sensitive. "Given that you just got out of something traumatic and so did she, you both didn't have time to heal. I know your intentions are good but you should've healed before you invited her to live with you."

My brother was right, I was trying to get myself together while helping her and still dealing with Ray. When it was time for us to go we were looking for Tahsa so she could go back home with us. We spent time with our Auntie Sally and Grandmother before we left, my Grandmother was outside and I was happy to see her. We went to Denny's for breakfast, it was good, I loved spending time with my family. My Aunt paid for our meal so we left a tip and we appreciated her for that. We definitely had a great time reminiscing and just being together still after you hear about people losing family due to the COVID-19. It was truly a blessing to see my family hearing my cousin Keith doing his thing with his podcast, check him out and download the Good News Sports app for Apple and Android, my brother being a policeman, just seeing everyone alive and well.

Meanwhile Tasha never made it to the airport we called, we waited, we almost missed our flight. We had to return back to work. I was very concerned then I wasn't because I said she's grown she knows what she is doing. When I got back I sent James a video expressing that I missed him. He replied, "How are you today?" "Pretty good I can't complain. Thanks for asking, how are you?" James didn't reply until two days later, "I am great just home chilling wyd?" "That's awesome, it would be better if I was there. I am at work." James didn't respond to that, I couldn't blame him, when I went to Vegas for a whole week without responding to his message. I am sure a million thoughts were going through his head. I honestly didn't want to talk to anyone while I was with my family, I haven't seen them in over 8 years. I missed them also, I was definitely living in the moment.

Shawn and I were still communicating. He was still trying to insist that I was in love with him because I was flirting. He was calling me sprung and I told him sex doesn't move me I need more than that to be sprung over a guy. December rolls around, Shawn and I are talking a lot. I got a room in December to spend time with Shawn, he never made it on time and instead of texting me that he wasn't going to make it, he made it seem like he was still coming. I was a little upset because I could have made other plans. I sent James a message late because I ended up falling asleep. James asked how long I was here until and I said, "Tonight." James never responded, to that I said, "I will be back soon, I have to do some packing and hopefully I can see you soon." "How was your stay?" James asked. I replied, "It was ok I went to drop my son off so I could pack and work. I am disappointed in myself for not reaching out to you. I was like maybe he'll call when he gets the message and I never sent it. But I needed that to get started with things, no more procrastination. I can get pleasure without putting in work first my punishment." I meant to say I can't get pleasure, but that was what I get. Trying to be a player, when I knew who I wanted all alone, I was just too scared it was too soon. I didn't want to feel something for someone if I didn't know if they felt the same way or not. Our conversions were light. James went to Denver, I told him to have fun and be safe. I guess I don't give the responses that he wants or normally receives. I wasn't always calling his phone, if he didn't text back right away, I didn't sweat him. James wasn't mine to sweat or get mad over that's how I viewed things.

Chapter 6

In the month of January I went to Vegas again, Sheena and I were going to go to the Poconos but we didn't. I felt like that was more for couples or a group of people rather than just us two going together. Although we could've gone skiing, Sheena has never been to the West

Coast. There's nothing better than experiencing that with someone who has been there numerous times before. First stop we go get the rental car, then the shop where we got edibles, got a Fat Tuesday then it was off to dinner at my favorite spot The Brass Fork. We had a good time, we walked the strip. I took her to Blueberry Hill, the food was awesome. We had mimosas just enjoying ourselves. It was all about us, this one guy followed us off the elevator. He said, "Y'all are just so beautiful this isn't even my floor, I was just looking at y'all and y'all made me forget where I was going." The guy was really cute but we really weren't on that type of time, it was a girls trip. I wanted her to enjoy herself and she did. Shawn video called me while I was out there normally I am at home chilling so I know it was a surprise I was out. Also I didn't post pictures nor shared our location. I really didn't want people to know I was in Vegas for the third time in less than a month. I just really went for her or else I wasn't taking that long flight again.

When we returned it was cold and Sheena kept saying, "West Coast me please." I agreed that the weather in Vegas was beautiful while we were still getting cold and snow. In the month of February, I barely spoke to James, I sent him some pics and told him to enjoy his weekend. I never got a response, until the 21st he texted,"Hi how have you been?" "I've been pretty good, thanks. What about you?" "I am great just working. What have you been up to lately?" "That's good, work, working out, writing and looking for a house. So a lot,what about you Mr. busy?" James didn't reply until March 4th saying, "Where are you looking for a house?" I didn't reply until March 6th, I am not good at being ignored, but who am I to feel any type of way when I took a whole week to reply to him while I was in Vegas. I texted him, "Lexington/Columbia. I will be down there this week. Maybe we can hangout." "Oh why do you want to move here?" "Family, and my son is down there, he doesn't even want to come back here. Plus there's nothing nor anyone here for me." James's response was, "Got you. That sounds like a plan. What you got going on today?" "Yes it definitely is. I'm at work right now, it's my last day! What about you?" No response until seven days later. "What have you been up to?" I waited a day, two can play at that game but I will win at this because I really don't give a spit. "Job interviews mainly you?"

Oh yea so I moved, I told Ray that I was going to South Carolina for my Mother's birthday but I really had a job interview. Ray left Bri's clothes at his place, even brand new clothes I just bought her. Ray said he would bring her bag of clothes tomorrow and I told him I will be leaving tomorrow. Little did he know I was leaving for good, so when he left her clothes it pissed me off because I knew I would have to buy her more clothes after just buying her new outfits. That was a sacrifice I was willing to take, anything to get away from this place. While being in Sc for a week Ray asked when were we going to return. I replied, "I will let you know when we do." I never did because I never returned.

Tasha and I went out for drinks, we were celebrating getting a new job. I texted James and asked him what he was doing tonight. James never answered so I called, I left a drunk voicemail on his phone. I don't remember what was said, all I know is I was embarrassed. James never called me back or texted me after the voicemail was left. I just let it and him go, one day Shawn called me wanting to meet up but it was a bad timing, my womanhood was taking its course so that was out. I saw a guy online that I used to work with Derrick, he was nice. We hung out a couple of times after work. I got a tattoo from his friend and he paid for it. I remember nothing but good vibes. We exchange numbers and begin to text. I have to go back to a time before I started hanging out with him again. I am working at a retirement center, so I am interacting with everyone and being friendly.

There is a guy there named BJ, he is handsome, he works with me, we just flirted with each other from time to time. There is this girl that was working there named Kay, she was saying things like he's trying to get me jealous it's not working. I was confused because when she wasn't even at work BJ would flirt with me so I knew he was not trying to make her jealous. This is how we always interact. BJ asked me for my number and I gave it to him. One day we go on break and then Kay runs outside. "Oh I thought you and BJ were on break together." I told her no, then she said, "It's not that I would care, just let me know if y'all are." I was like ok if she didn't care then why do I have to let her know. Alright so moving forward she invites me to go out with her for drinks to talk etc. I should've known there was a motive behind it but I was being nice because she was already disliked by almost everyone we worked with. When we get settled and get our drinks and food she starts to talk about work. I told her everyone isn't your friend and I also wanted to inform her that people are saying you have bad breath but they don't know how to tell you, myself included. Kay gets mad and says, "Who said that BJ he's the only one that got close to me?" Kay called BJ while we were there. Kay walked outside to talk to him, when she came back in she started getting her stuff to leave. She said that BJ said I was talking about her too, which I was, I told her to her face that I agreed that her breath was smelling. I just didn't know how to tell her, especially because I didn't know her like that. Well she caused a scene at the place we were at, the server came over and asked, "Is everything ok?" Kay told the server that I am paying for her drink. I said, "No, she can pay for her own drink." I did offer to buy her drink before she acted like a child instead of hearing the words that were said to her. I also told her she was still a child. She said, "I'm a grown woman baby, trust me." Kay left me all by myself, I stayed and finished my drink.

I saw a friend that I used to work with there. I used to sleep at his house when I had to get up early in the morning, so I didn't have to drive all the way to the Northeast side of town. His name is Aaron, what's crazy is Aaron knows James they played football together in High School and College. Also Aaron has been with one of my sisters so that's out I don't do that. Aaron and I are out having a good time drinking, dancing as friends, just vibing. Aaron was looking at other girls and guys were looking at me. I really was just about having fun taking my mind off what just transpired. We stayed out until about 2 a.m. We were about to go to Waffle House but they were switching shifts so it was an hour wait. I decided to go home. I went to sleep since I had to work in the morning. The next day at work, Kay showed up, she told her side of the story to the manager and went home she said she didn't feel comfortable working. The manager Mrs. King came up to me and asked what happened between y'all and I told her, "I was trying to tell her what everyone is too afraid to tell her but she took it the wrong way." Mrs. King said, "Yea because I was trying to give her a scenario and I asked her, are you the type of person that gets mad when something is being said to you?" The manager said Kay got upset saying, "No I don't do that." So she basically proved my point. I wasn't even mad at Kay for what she did and I didn't blame her for disliking me. I learned to not take things personally and that some people don't love themselves, so that's how they have to go about things to get validation. Sis don't be mad when someone doesn't like you they really don't like themselves that goes for the fellas too. It's so sad we live in a world where if someone is doing better than you or looks better than you, you already hate the person in your mind. Also you must be doing something right to even get noticed like that. Let your haters be your biggest motivators, I know I do HI HATERS!

The whole thing was she was trying to see if I was messing around with Bj. I didn't although, we would flirt just to pass time. We would text every now and then. We were going to hang out when I was off from work but I had to go to Delaware to move my things. Also I just never had time, one day the girl Kay and this other coworker Angela got into an argument. They already didn't like each other so this time things got really wild. I guess Kay felt like no one liked her because of Angela. This is how it started, the manager Mrs. King said, "Before I leave I want to know that everyone is going to do their job with no attitudes. We are going to help no matter whose section it is." Kay said, "I don't have a problem with that." Then she called out Angela and said, "She put silverware on everyone else's section but mine." After that everything was trick this trick that. I beat your ass imma draw blood trick, I was like wow they were trying to get to each other. They threw chairs, Kay went outside to go around to get to Angela, it was a disaster. They both got fired for almost fighting. If I was going to get fired I would've at least got a lick in but by then again I don't do all that talking when it comes to fighting. I just want the person to run up, I save all of my energy for the fight not the pre fight just saying. Not too long after the whole gang was split up, there was this guy from New York who rubbed me the wrong way. I'm just coming out of a traumatic relationship so they way people talked to me I wasn't having it. I knew he could've beat my ass but I didn't care I told him off I don't care who you are or what you could do to me at this point I wasn't taking no bs.

The guy was just rough when he talked very aggressively and had an attitude, for no reason like he got mad because he almost splashed water on me. I was like really it's just water then he said, "No you probably would go tell that I did it on purpose." I didn't have a reason to do that so I told him to chill. Then I was joking with him one day, then he snapped so I told him, I was joking and you need to calm all the way down. Then I just stopped talking to him all together. Jack got fired, I was happy I guess for a while, then I just was tired of working everyday. It was taking up too much of my time. There was this girl I worked with named Amy, she's very nice. She has three kids, she takes care of them with the help of her mother, she's a hard worker. One day we go on break together and her boyfriend calls her. This guy is so disgusting he was accusing her of having sex with someone on her break. Amy tried to give me the phone, to tell him she wasn't with anyone else but me. I told her no because he's not going to like what I have to say. That's how Ray was so I had a ptsd moment and I was about to snap. If you have to prove to a man that you're not doing anything and they keep accusing you, that's their guilty conscience eating away at themselves. I just didn't have the energy for that because he also disrespects his mother and yells at Amy. I told Amy, "You could do better, you don't need that in your life." Also Mrs. King was starting to get on my nerves so I felt like I can only take so much in a workplace. My peace of mind was more important than money can buy so I left that place. While I was working there I do recall a guy from Dss family services contacted me for an emergency custody hearing for my daughter Bri. I knew this was coming, I just didn't know when.

Chapter 7

Ray was filing for custody for Bri. The guy from Dss Mr. Green was happy that I answered the phone or else everything would've been in Ray's favor. Mr. Green was very helpful to me, he asked me questions and I was completely honest with him. Even things that I was too embarrassed to admit, but I would rather tell him the truth. Then for him to find out. Mr. Green wanted to see Bri also where she slept. Ray said that my life was in danger and also Bri's life. I shared something about my family's past and he used that against me. It was very hurtful, the things he said. Ray also brought up the fact that I had an abortion that made me snap. That was something I was trying to forgive myself for. I wasn't proud of it at the end of the day, heartbeat or not it was still a part of me. I suffered great depression after all that transpired and he was trying to pick at old wounds. Ray really used my past hurt to attack me, but he would get mad when I called him a bum. Well if he knew he wasn't a bum then he would not have gotten offended. I just saw him for who he really was and he didn't like it.

Mr. Green wants what's best for Bri and myself so he advised me to reach out to a Domestic violence liaison. Let me tell y'all when I recalled things I went through I cried and I almost regurgitated everything I ate that morning. The liaison asked me a series of questions. I start to remember things I tried to forget. This one question stuck out to me: "Have you ever been forced to perform a sexual act without your consent?" Yes there was a time when I was staying at Ray's mother's house. Ray and I were intimate and Bri was laying in the bed with us sleeping. I told Ray I don't feel comfortable doing that with my daughter in the bed. I didn't care if she was sleeping, that's disgusting. Ray didn't care because one night I woke up to him putting his manhood inside of me from the back. Bri was laying down next to me, I could see her face, so I closed my eyes until he finished. I cried myself to sleep that night. I was so numb to how he was treating me, I also felt like I had to endure this hardship to get to work. I had other people to help me but I couldn't put that on them. They had nothing to do with my downfall and the one that is responsible for it took full advantage of me. Ray had no respect for me nor his own daughter. I left and went to Carl's house, I just didn't feel comfortable there anymore, I stayed for one night then I had to leave. I appreciated Carl for being there for me, I needed that time away. Like I said I couldn't ask him to go out his way for me I didn't feel right. Carl would have to pass up his job to take me to work then come back to work, then pick me up again, then come back that's just too much. That was a traumatic moment for me with Ray, I definitely tried to forget it, but it was brought up when I spoke to the Domestic Violence Liaison. I cried again just thinking about how sick he was. Also she asked a series of questions and she gave me a score at the end. She said to me, "Did you know your life was in Danger? All of the ones you answered yes to caused your life to be in danger." I was shocked like I really made it out because you don't hear that everyday. I was just tired of not being happy. I am grateful I made it out and alive Hallelujah!!

While I was still working at the retirement home, my parents helped me move my things from Delaware to South Carolina. It was perfect timing because my baby sister was just about to move into her place. I was able to just move my furniture etc into her place. I ended up moving in with my parents so I could get back on my feet. I definitely did not want to, but I had to swallow my pride. Finically I wasn't where I used to be. I could have had a down payment on a house by now, especially with all the money I wasted on and with Ray. Another thing that was brought up by the Domestic Violence liaison, he controlled my finances. That's a sign of abuse as well as the other things she listed. I was also served paperwork for the hearing and when I got to Delaware I saw

Sheena. Sheena was reading all the lies he was telling and she said, "Why is he lying yo?" I replied, "He's crazy." Just to sum up everything he was lying about he said that I was sleeping with married men, also I leave my kids alone all the time and I have a record with Dss stating that I left them alone. Of course he mentioned I was on drugs and it came from me receiving the stimulus checks. How? When I had to pay to get my car fixed, with that money and the money I saved from my income tax. Also I have been to Vegas more than once and I only checked on Bri once since I went to Vegas. Nothing was relevant to the safety of Bri. Also I don't leave my kids at home alone, Tasha was there to help before that it was Sheena.

After the emergency hearing it was put in place that Bri speaks to Ray three times a week via video chat. Also she was to spend a week with him Saturday to Saturday at the end of each month. The plan he had to take me down didn't work. We have another court date for the custody case. The first time we had to meet Ray, I didn't go, I had to work so I paid my parents to meet for the exchange. When my parents returned my Dad said he took a long time to get there, Ray just didn't have respect for people and their time. My Dad also said, "He is using the woman that he was with because she looks really old." My response was, "I really don't care, she doesn't know who he is yet." I really didn't care but I felt sorry for her, she really didn't know what she walked herself and son into. I am guessing she is just tired of the run around and settled for him. Ray would have you feeling like you're the only one meanwhile he will be talking to countless others and then lie to you about who they are. When Ray was calling Mia he lied and said, that's how he makes money, he has to call that number then money goes into his account. I never believed that, also this idiot would call her on the house phone like there wasn't a caller ID. Ray put me through what I allowed him to. If I didn't have the power to walk away, he would still be doing the same things. I would make excuses for how he treated me. Half the time I thought it was my fault because I didn't know how to love correctly. That could not have been true because since I started living with my parents I began to see how love was really supposed to be. They have been married for 35 years and they still love each other. They joke around with each other, communicate, they just complete each other.

I wasn't in a rush to find a new job, I had more healing to do. While I was working at the retirement home I rekindled a fling. Deon, we have history chemistry, history, and esp so Deon sent me a message in 2014 I never replied why? Real life loyal chick until the end, Deon understood so we proceeded with talking. Deon would text me almost every morning, I loved it. We finally met up and when we did I was nervous to be honest. Deon was no longer the young boy that I used to know, he's a full grown man. Deon and I began to converse about the past, he said, "I remember when you were all on me and they said y'all in love you couldn't stay off of me." I asked if he remembered Boone and he did. I told him she passed away. We all hung out in the past Deon said, "I remember getting to your place, I just don't know how I got there.I know we had a good time, you're a whole vibe." While we are reminiscing of the past he recalls something that I did for him that no girl or woman has ever topped and he challenged me to it. Deon looked me in the eyes when he asked so, looked in his eyes and said, "Yes" it has been a while since I've been intimate, I went right alone and did it. "Damn you weren't lying," he stated, we were talking about past situations where we tried with people but it didn't work. I told him about James just a little bit, I mainly talked about Ray because of the last book. Deon said, "It was crazy when you hit me up because it was a New Moon and I was just thinking about how you were doing." I was like, "What do you know about the New Moon?" He said, "I've been researching and studying about the different origins of the book." I thought that was mad dope for real could it be fate and timing couldn't be even better. I wasn't really searching for something real, I just wanted something to feel. I did have opportunities but I didn't want them. One thing about me is if I am going to be intimate with someone, it has to be meaningful. I am a frequent visitor of my past, I always go back to people I spoke to once before or been with once before. Deon was one of them, Deon and I would text ever now and then.

Meanwhile this guy Derrick I used to work with him. We decided to hangout so we went to eat at a Caribbean restaurant. It was good, we talked and caught up on life. Derrick and I hugged, he was trying to see me again but I went to Florida, for my uncle's funeral. It was a really sad moment for me because I haven't been going to family reunions since I've been with Ray. That made me realize life is too short to be wasting time with someone who doesn't value family. I can't get back the time I lost while being with him. The things I missed out on, it wasn't worth it, I was living with regret. Speaking of living with regrets I was out celebrating getting a new job this is before I left my job. Tasha and I went out, yes she was back from Vegas it was surely a blessing she had been through a lot, we forgive each other for the past hurt we might have caused each other. I was just happy to see her after what she had been through. That's not my story to tell, she will probably share it one day, I just know she's blessed. I got drunk and called James, I was in my feelings and I needed someone to hold me, or rather I just wanted someone to hold me. I remember saying I don't want to see your face and why are we playing games we are too old for this.

James never called, texted or responded to my voicemail. He liked my picture though I got tired of seeing that he would be on Facebook and not reply to me. So I deleted him, out of sight and out of mind. Not really although I tried to escape him and how I was feeling for him but he was still in my dreams. So one day I took it upon myself to go to his job, especially since I texted him a long paragraph: "Hey James I just want to start off saying I apologize for leaving that message on your phone and saying things that I really don't remember which is embarrassing for me.. I also want to thank you for encouraging me to write. There were times when I was in South Carolina and I would get a room and I wrote when I didn't see you and I would fall asleep. So thank you for that too, I needed that time to myself. I don't know if your posts were pertaining to me but they did help me and inspired me to push and do better, also to be better. Not for people but for myself. I appreciate you for that. I am happy you came into my life, even if it was just for a season. I hope all is well.." James's response was, "Idk what massage you talking about. I don't really check my messages like that so it's all good glad I can help. How have you been ?" "Lol ok cool I'm happy to hear that.. I've been better.. I just been working and writing.. hanging out with my family.. how have you been ?" "Where are you working at now?" I told him where I work and he reiterated where he worked as if I didn't already know for sure although he already posted it on his page numerous times. I guess those were signs for me to visit while I was in town, I just never got the clue. Hence why I posted, "No one has time for these Blues Clues games just say what you want.. It's that simple." I have been talking about popping up on him when we first started talking but I thought that would be awkward. I don't like showing up to places if I'm not invited. I felt this was the perfect time to show my face. I was so nervous and I didn't want to go alone, so Tasha came alone with me. I didn't see his car so I had Tasha call his job to see if he was there, he was. My heart was pounding so hard, I went to Publix to buy some flowers for him.

When we arrived he was by the door and he didn't even recognize me. I said oh this is sweet lol James asked if we wanted to go to the bar or a table? I answered, "Wherever your section is." Then I gave him the flowers and said, "This is for you." James looked so confused like really, then Tasha said, "You don't know who she is?" She told me to take my mask off and I said "No I don't know him like that." he said, "Oh wow I can't tell with these masks on. How are you doing?" He asked while giving me a hug. I told him I was well, then he sat down in the booth with me while putting his arm around me, rubbing on my arm, I didn't think all that was going to happen. I asked him why he was playing games? I stated, If I wanted to play games, I have Call of Duty on my Ps4 for that. James was looking fine like always and I was getting hot idk if it was him or the drink I had. We chatted as much as we could, he was busy. James was nice enough to give us Fifty percent off the bill, then he mentioned he should've paid for the whole meal. James made time to walk us outside, he gave me a nice hug, I wanted to kiss him because I really did miss him. In the restaurant he asked. "Why did I move here?" I do remember telling him for my family and my son, I guess he wanted me to say it was for him. Slightly that was a reason but mainly for the fam, I would never base my decision on a man again. James texted, "Thanks for the flowers." I really needed to show my appreciation to him because he was my inspiration, my motivation. I wouldn't be where I am today if it wasn't for him being a positive vibe in my life so that was the least I could do was show him that I appreciated him. I confronted him about his post but he shied away from saying anything. I feel like I acknowledged it too late. One of his friend's knew something or someone was making him post a lot, they said, "Bestfriend you need to call me." Even if he denied it was about me I didn't care, it helped me get through my darkest moment.

That night I decided to go out with my friend Derrick, we went to Social. We had a good time, we took shots and we passed the hookah. I really enjoyed myself, I was finding out that's what life was all about. Although I just took James flowers I decided to hang out, it wasn't like I was in a relationship. I really just wanted to show my appreciation to him. I'm single so I'm definitely mingling. It took awhile to get here but I'm loving it. I am not in a rush to settle down. If it happens it happens, if it doesn't hey I'm still here for my kids and family. James and I texted for a while after that then two days went by I did not reply, I was really busy. After that James didn't reply at all, until I went to see Deon, I met his cousin and he was really chilled down to earth. We all were talking, having a very intellectual conversation, I did speak to them about James. They gave me some insight from a male perspective, so I understood how James might have felt and how I made him feel that way. Either way I wanted to know, I knew that I liked him, I just didn't want him to know how much. I wasn't ready to because I was unsure if he felt the same way or he didn't. Although I was there with Deon I was talking about James. Deon did say, "Soul ties." That could be a good and bad thing, that's why you have to watch who you give yourself to, some people don't have the intent to stay. That can drive you crazy wondering if it's something wrong with you or if you did something wrong. After Deon, his cousin and I conversed, his cousin left, so we were intimate, it was like he was trying to make a statement. Deon definitely did make his statement loud and clear. When I arrived home I told him I appreciate him for his time because I knew he is a busy man but he took time out of his schedule to see me. Deon said, "I appreciate you too and hopefully you have some inspiration." I replied with a picture of my laptop. "Most definitely, I am watching family matters and writing thanks." "Yes ma'am you know we are good." "Indeed very good." I really was inspired, I wrote a few chapters of this book because he inspired me not just sexually but intellectually. Although I was feeling Deon he didn't deserve to have half of me. My mind and body was still stuck on James, I am still not working so I decided to apply for a job in Downtown Columbia.

I did not realize how close it was to where James worked, I was nervous about that. I got the job, before I started working I decided to take a little vacay to Charlotte NC. My sister, her boyfriend at the time and I, we stayed at Drury Suites. Hands down the best place I have ever stayed and that's a lot, when I was homeless we stayed in numerous hotels. Drury had breakfast, snack time, dinner and two free adult beverages. It was so good, it also had an indoor pool and a jacuzzi, we had a good time. I went bowling with Tasha and her boyfriend. Yes I didn't have a date it was me,myself and I and that was fine because I'm enough and I love myself. Once you realize that you can have fun and enjoy life without having to have someone around you will really start living life for real. Yes it gets lonely at times, but you're still alive so there is hope that you can find someone to enjoy your life with. While I was out there I did see Deon, we just talked, I told him about how my job was close to where James worked. Deon said, we were "meant to be," I told him that I didn't think so if a guy wants you in their life they would make it so. I really felt like I just needed closure and an understanding of why when I was 528 miles away I saw James more than I did when I was only 5 miles away. I also had a massage appointment with N.T.A. It was amazing and it was also my selfcare day and second time getting a massage from N.T.A. The guy Dana was amazing and very professional. If you're ever in the Charlotte area, South Carolina and Atlanta area book him you will not be disappointed. N.T.A will come to you Dana travels he's also a personal trainer if you want to get in shape.

I went to James' place of work again after I was done training at my job, I walked and I took my laptop so that I can work on this book. I see him when I walk in he says, "You can't just be popping up at my job like this." I said it's a public place, James said, "True." Then I said, "I can leave if you want me to?" He said, "Nah you good." Then he mentioned he wasn't a server anymore he was a manager. I said, "Awww congrats." Then he suggested I sit at the bar, I said no because I wanted to finish up some chapters of this book. I ordered food and a drink, James sat in the booth with me he had his arm around me. I asked him, "For real, what's going on?" " I am talking to someone." I was like I, "Oh ok you could've told me I would understand. Me out of all people." James said, "It's nothing serious." I told him, "It must be if you can't spend time with me, talk to me or text me." Then he said, "We could still be friends, text me sometimes, you're out here your son is happy he's with his friend you have your family." I said, "You're right I am alive, I made it out of my situation with the help of you. You told me to move in silence and that's all I could think of doing until I did it." I tried to hide the hurt in my voice but it did hurt, it made me feel like what we shared wasn't special. In spite of all that I was grateful for James being in my life, he really did inspire me the most. I did mess up trying to be a player or just trying to keep my guard up. It was just so hard to let my guard down after what I've been through and I was free falling into someone else so fast so I was scared.

James paid for my food then I waited for a little while to tell him thank you but he never came back. I decided to text him. "Thanks for the food, I will see you around." James didn't reply, so I felt like that chapter of my life was closed, I was grateful for what I gained from that. Strength, courage, wisdom and confidence. As I began working I did lose interest in wanting to spend time with someone so I just started focusing on myself. I was working out more, I was spending more time with my kids just staying focused on myself. I can admit it was getting boring and being involuntary celibate wasn't working for me. I am also picky with who I give myself to so it wasn't so easy to just go out there. One day out of the blue I am coming into work I see this handsome man named Rick, he's mixed, he has lighted colored eyes, very sexy, he introduced himself, then he left he was just getting off. While I was cleaning up my last table preparing to leave. Rick came in "Hey Marie so how's it going?" I said "Pretty good thanks." He said , "That's good," as I was leaving out I forgot his name so I asked my coworker then I said, "See you later Rick." he replied, "Have a good one sweetie." I said, "Thanks, you too." and went home, I still want to build something with someone so I get on Plenty of fish. I am not really interested in the people who were trying to talk to me. You will not believe who I do see online, Mr. James, I guess he really wasn't serious about whoever he was talking to. I didn't care, I still didn't text him his loss I feel like. James also mentioned he didn't want anything serious; he likes his own time and space. All that was understandable to me, I was trying to give him that. Honestly I told him he opened Pandora's box then shut it tight with no explanation. I was too good at just being friends with someone and not having too many emotions behind it. I guess guys don't like that, I explained that I move according to how the other person moves, I try to match people's energy. I just felt better now that I knew it wasn't me that caused us to lose our connection. I didn't like it but hey that's life, and it must go on. Besides, what happened next boosted your girl's self esteem to the roof. I had put James in the back of my mind so I was doing things to distract myself from him working out, singing on this app on my phone, everything but writing because at the moment I was still stuck on the part about James. I began reminiscing so all I wanted again was what we had, it wasn't anything serious to me. I just really enjoyed his company.

Chapter 8

As I am hustling making my money at work Rick is flirting with me, I thought nothing of it because he's young I ask him his age he's only 21 years olds I know right. How Marie got her groove back. One day we are working and he asks me for my number so I give it to him. We began chatting daily, "Hey beautiful." Rick stated "Hey handsome." I replied "You're so fine." Rick stated "You are too what are we going to do with each other lol rhetorical question." I said "It's your world, I'm just living in it." Was Rick's reply "That's dope, well we shall have fun." I said "I hope so." Said Rick "Indeed." "You are clever." Rick said "I know this lol." Then Rick said to me, "You the devil." I replied "Not at all I don't have pride." "You're very interesting, I like that." I'm feeling our vibe so far." I texted him in the a.m "Grand rising handsome have a wonderful day." "You too love." Rick replied "Thanks." "Ugh you are too fine I'm really attracted to your vibe." I appreciate the compliment so I said, "Thanks you are too! I like looking into your eyes, they're beautiful." Rick said "You can stare at em' as long as you want." "Thanks it will be my pleasure." "Sooooo about this cuddle session." "Yes, what about it?" "When do you wanna come over?" Rick asked, "Whenever you get off and get settled." "Ok bet." Rick didn't message me back until the next day saying, "Good morning" I replied back. I believe another week went by we saw each other at work, we would flirt all shift. It was the anticipation for me, when I was off and Rick was off we decided to finally meet up. I went to his place and we were watching Pooty Tang, that set the mood for fun and that's what we had fun. Rick gave me a back massage, it was very relaxing. Then I gave him one, of course we were intimate. I enjoyed myself after that I went back home and he told me to let him know when I made it. I did and I was surprised he was still up to reply. I was happy and it was what I needed right before my trial for custody.

One day I dropped Bri off and picked her up from the meeting place. I also saw the woman Ray was with, to me she was nice looking, I don't do that hater stuff. At the end of the day I left him, I just never introduced myself to her because Ray is way too dramatic so the most I did was give her a smile. I would take that drive with my sister's brother in law, he was really nice for taking that trip with me. I appreciated him for that, we did try to work something out but he lives in Virginia so that was out. I was getting prepared to hit all the key points to take Ray down. I knew that I was already in favor of the court because Ray lied about his criminal past to the DSS worker. Although they already had the proof in front of their face. That's Ray, he would lie and deny, even with evidence presented to him. Court is in session, Ray gets to go first which I am happy about because I get to write down the lies he was telling the judge. Ray speaks about how my daughter's hair is never done,(false I always do her hair and when he was living with me he would say he's going to take her to a professional to get her hair done.) Also he puts fear in Bri, when she gets her hair done by me. Ray traumatized her since she was 3 years old, he would freak out because she was crying. Bri didn't like getting her hair washed, I started doing her hair when he wasn't there and we didn't have a problem. Another thing Ray mentioned was when he picked her up her panties would be dirty, it was a light mark in her panties it wasn't even brown. Ray said we didn't wipe her good and she had poop stains in her panties. Well after riding for 8 hours I don't expect anyone wearing white underwear to have them spotless. Ray was just all emotional, my emotions were out of it I really just was speaking facts. I explained what I went through being with him of course he tried to interrupt. I told the judge about when my daughter and I were kicked out. We were placed into a homeless shelter although I was working and willing to pay his mother rent money, until I found a place to stay. The Judge was very interested to hear what happened next, I wanted to say I wrote a book about it, it's on amazon but no I just continued on until I explained why I moved. I was working two jobs at the time so the judge said well you are at work a lot so the grandfather will really be the one there.

I told her yes for now until school starts because I knew I would have to be there for the kids. I was scared I was hoping that didn't affect her decision. They went on break for about 5 minutes to make a decision, the Judge asked Ray what he wanted of course he was selfish with his answer he wanted full custody of Bri. The judge asked me what I wanted, I said I want her to have a relationship with her father, he can see her on school breaks etc. I was shaking waiting for the answer, I won custody at the end of it all. Ray texted and said he's filing for an appeal. I was happy, then it was like damn I still have to deal with him. I will tell everyone be careful who you lay with if you can't see a future with them then don't even do it. It shouldn't matter how horny you are, just go play with yourself or practice self control. To have power over something that seems to have the power over most human beings is incredible. After that was all said and done it was time to celebrate, in spite of the fact that Ray wanted to rain on our parade. I bought pizza and cupcakes to celebrate, went to my little sis house, played music and had a good time. I didn't tell my daughter why we had a party, I did tell her you will be living with me. Also told her she will be going to school with her brother and cousin, she was excited about that. I was happy I went through so much already with being around Ray's family emotional, financial, and spiritual torment.

After the case Ray still would call and make smart remarks about me to my daughter. Bri said,"Daddy my tablet is dead." Ray's response was, "I don't know why mommy wont charge your tablet I keep telling her charge your tablet." Ray repeated that, so my Daughter being the smart girl I raised said, "Daddy I can charge my own tablet." boom freaking weirdo. Ray would also constantly lie to Bri Daddies coming to get you soon. Then I finally told Bri, you will see your Dad when school is on break. Ray was definitely playing physics games on his own daughter, he's pathetic. Ray would also have conversations with my daughter telling her. "You're not at home, home is when you have your own room." At times I can admit, I ended their phone conversations really quickly. This guy had nothing nice to say. Like we weren't sleeping in a car on cold winter nights and I begged him to let me and Bri go to SC. I told him to work and save up to get a place. Ray was the reason why I couldn't get a place, he didn't pay his 200 dollars car note. When the car was in my name so please don't do that. Remember where you came from and who helped get you there. I am humble enough to start over, I know that I am willing to provide my kids with the best. Back to the work scene, Rick and I are working together flirting as usual. I am minding my own business working and I feel someone staring at me. Y'all will not believe who I see with his baby momma, Ant. So you know what I did next I went to the table and said, "What's up? Hey, how are you doing Ant? Aww is this your little girlfriend? How cute." No I didn't, I just continued working as if I never saw him. I had to walk by their table because my tables were in the same area. I could feel him staring, I never acknowledged him, even when they left. I could have caused a scene because he hurt me, but it wasn't worth it and I was over it. It's funny to me that he came to my job. Ant and I went to my job before I started working here. That's when he met my friends. I believe it was his first time being there. Now he's taking her to places we've been together. I mean the food is good so I know he was there for that. What were the chances of him actually running into me there. No one knew I moved, I never posted where I worked. It was just a mere coincidence. It was all good I was happy for him. I was happy for myself because I let him go. I refused to be a second option or woman in a man's life. I loved myself too much for that crap.

Rick and I decided to hangout after work so I waited for him to get off then I headed to his place where we talked etc. I told Rick about Ant and how he was there with his baby momma, how he lied about her existence just to get with me. After the night was over I went home, Rick was just a chapter of my life he helped me get back out there but also to keep my guard up. Don't confuse a good time with a lifetime, I was able to control my emotions. Although I liked him, not only for what he did to me physically, but for him he had ambition, goals, and a bright future. Rick is young and he has a whole future to look forward to. Rick and I would still chat but I knew it wasn't going anywhere. I decided to get on a dating app but I was looking to market so I can make more sales on my book. This one guy stood out to me, so we chatted online for a while until we exchanged numbers and when we did we talked non stop. Brandon is his name, we would facetime and everything, he was in Miami and didn't get back to Columbia until the end of the week so we were getting to know each other. When Brandon got back in town he came over, we talked in his truck because I don't like people meeting my family especially if they don't have intentions to stay. I guess I'm different because he took me to his place and I met his sister, niece, and brother in law. Awkward as hell to me, but hey whatever I was spending time with him that's all that mattered. I felt like this is going to be it, I can just talk to one guy again. Sike for real not saying we just stopped talking we still do but we just don't see each other as much as we used to it's all good because what happens next is pretty dope.

Chapter 9

I got a message from someone I used to work with in Security. We were supposed to be meeting at Stars and Stripes. It was changed to a restaurant, guess which restaurant he chose. The one that James works at no lie you can't make this up. I hesitated on going because I haven't spoken to him since he told me he was talking to someone. I didn't want him to think I was stalking him. I could've, I had the address to his house that's just not me. Also I always saw him working in the mornings so I was like what are the chances he would be there at night. I was drinking wine before I got to the restaurant because I was so nervous. When I arrived we were standing outside waiting for more people to show up but I had to use the restroom and good thing I did because as soon as we walked in James was at the hostess stand. So I zoomed past and went to the restroom. We got seated, I sat in a spot so that James could see me, also I wanted to sit close to my sister. No one knew I moved back so I surprised a few people. We really had a great time, I'm sure James saw me but he didn't come over and say anything I didn't expect him to, I was with a group of people he didn't know. I was alright with that, I was so tipsy, I was feeling good. I had to use the restroom a lot so I stopped by my job to use the restroom. My sis Tasha and I decided to go out, we were supposed to go to Social but something happened, so we didn't go. So we decided to go to Greens. It's a 25 and up place. I love it because they play music I actually know, old school, a little new and sometimes that island groove.

The vibes there were off the chain, I saw Aaron there. Remember he was intimate with my older sister so I saw him strictly as a friend. We were all dancing with Aaron, Tasha and I. I saw this guy, he caught my eye maybe because he was just vibing to the music. Also I saw him whispering to his friend and looking at me so I decided to help him out and also myself. I did a 360 around Aaron and then I was closer to the guy, he took me by the hand for some reason I was nervous, so then I turned around. The guy was smelling so nice, I knew that I was interested, he had clean shoes, a beard of course that just turns me on. We were dancing close and for the rest of the night he wanted to walk me to my car so I said, "No" then he insisted so I said, "Ok." "Look you parked right next to me so you know it's meant to be." I chuckled because no matter what he had to go that way to his truck. When he walked me to my car we talked, and hugged, I was about to fall asleep in his arms. "You're going to make me take you home." He said then he asked, "Do you think your sister would mind if I take you home?" I'm like you didn't even ask if I mind. He gets my number and tells me his name Leroy. I told Leroy to follow me to my sister's place so that I can drop my car off, Leroy suggested that he drive since it was late, I didn't object I went along with it.

Leroy is driving and we are talking while listening to music for at least 30 mins, he lives far away from my house and Tasha's spot. As we pull up to his house I am shocked like wow he opened the garage door. I stepped out of the truck and then I walked in his house and I assumed I had to whisper because someone else was in the house because it was pretty big for just one person. Then he asked, "Would you like to sleep in the bed or on the couch whatever is comfortable for you?" I said, "It doesn't matter, so we went to the room." He said he's been wanting to do something all night and he kissed me. The way Leroy kissed me was like he already knew me. Like he knew what I liked, I wasn't the type to go home with a guy on the first night but how everything transpired it just felt so right. I really didn't think that Leroy would be so consistent but he was. That night was amazing, it continued into the morning, then I showered he did as well. Then Leroy had to get ready to drop a bouncy house off to someone, seeing him work hard was a turn on. I couldn't lift those bean bags because they were really heavy. I felt like a woman when I was around him it was just so natural. Singing Natural woman by Aretha Franklin real talk, I was loving it. The very same day he texted me we were texting all night while I was at work. Leroy's birthday was on a

Sunday so I texted him happy birthday. I had to work, so I rested until then we texted on Sunday, then Monday I was off so he called me and we talked on the phone for an hour. Basically this man was doing everything right calling, texting, and staying consistent so I decided to cook for him. I made flank steak, sweet potatoes, mac n cheese, and cornbread. A man that works as hard as he does deserve a home cooked meal. I went to Leroy's house, we drank wine, talked and ate dinner while watching House Party, the atmosphere was set. We enjoyed ourselves, I discovered he had a speaker so I connected and played my playlist. It was on from there, I told him I was going home so he could sleep, he said, "It's too late for you to go home." It really wasn't but I knew he wanted me to stay and so did I. I normally don't stay the night at guys house but his vibe made me feel so comfortable. I would make up a lame excuse like I have to take my fish for a walk just to leave. Or I would text my sister to call me like it's an emergency.

We cuddled for a while then fell asleep, I helped Leroy get up because his alarm went off a while ago. When he made it to work he let me know, I am not going to keep speaking about him I want to see how this goes. One more thing while I was at work he left a note on my car saying: "Hope you had a great night at work. I just wanted to leave this note for you. Hoping it puts a smile on your face, and ends your night with a warm heart. Your Friend Leroy p.s. you know you really didn't do any work lol" and yes it did make me smile really hard, I was so happy to see that note. I've been with Ray for six years and he never did anything sweet like that for me and he was an alleged "writer." A quote said; *"A person in two months can make you feel what a person in two years couldn't. Time means nothing, character does."* Leroy is a really nice guy from what I see so far we shall see where things go from here. Well you see this loving after chaos book was all about me loving myself enjoying myself. Enjoying my time with my kids trying to get myself together health and fitness praying and meditating. You have to become who you want to attract. If you want someone positive, be positive. If you want someone to motivate you, be motivational. Start with yourself, speak life into yourself, love yourself everything else will fall into place when you least expect it. I am fully healed from my past, I definitely feel incontrol of my future, I felt better and more confident when I stepped back on the dating scene. I am going to just tell you a series of times that I spoke life into people's lives and it came true. I'm not saying I'm a guru or genie, nothing like that but the word does say when two or more are gathered in my name. Alright so first one that I could remember, this girl I worked with at the hospital in security let's call her Sade. Sade was trying to get pregnant, she was asking my sister for help and I was giving her pointers as well. Then I said, "Watch when you do get pregnant you will probably have twins then you're not going to know what to do." Sade and I fell out due to an altercation we had at work so we were no longer friends on Facebook. Years later she added me back and I saw that she had twin boys. True story, my next one was my friend Hector. Hector we worked to get at Red Lobster in Delaware he was so hung up on this girl Mary, she was out of his league compared to the guys she talked to. I told Hector, "Forget her you'll meet someone soon that will like you and then you'll run to me and tell me all about it. I believe like a week or so later Hector came to me and said, "Marie you will not believe what happened to me." I am smiling because he is smiling then I'm like, "What?" Hector tells me he met someone they stayed on the phone, until the sun rose and he hasn't done that since high school. I was so happy for him. They are now married and have a beautiful baby together. Another encounter was with my coworker Anita, we worked together as well. Anita wanted to be a teacher so she was telling me she was scared. I told her don't be you already got the job. Anita said, "You think so?" I said, "I know so you just have to believe it yourself." The most high works in mysterious ways, Anita ended up serving one of the ladies who was a part of the school district and so she put in a great recommendation. Y'all already why I'm telling you that she got the job of course.

My favorite manager, I saw her at the gas station, she said she was tired. She was doing General manager things but wasn't the Gm. I told her, "your hard work will pay off soon." She said, "I hope so." I said, "It will, watch your name, will be on a building one day. You already know though, it happened so fast after I spoke to her. Sheena called me and asked, "Are you going to Red Lobster?" I replied "For what?" "Zoe's going away party she's moving to Scranton she has a GM position there." I went, of course that right there made me smile hard, I really believed that great things would happen for people just not myself at that time. Well I never spoke to the person about this. Although I did have dreams that a childhood brother of mine would be free from prison and we were at church and he would testify about how he made it through. He's free now and I am grateful for that. My mindset has changed for the better, I think positive thoughts. We have to speak life into our lives and everyone around us. I was able to travel when I cut free from Ray, I went to Atlanta. My lil sis, who is my son's Auntie, went there for her birthday. I was happy to see the family and we had a good time. My lil sister Dee has a song out Can't be the One Devour My Persuasion on all music platforms. I alway knew she had talent, she just actually put in the work and got it done. I was also able to see my beautiful Aunt get married, I cried at the wedding the second one I cried at. Just that little push of encouragement can go a long way for some people, even when I was in my chaos I still believed things would get better for other people. James was that person for me the Most High will use anyone as a vessel we just have to take heed to the lesson. I met someone I wasn't looking for, Leroy has brought me so much joy and laughter in my life in such a short period of time, I feel I don't deserve it sometimes. Leroy is really a great guy, he works two jobs, he has ambition and goals. Most of all he's treating me right so far, so we will see where it goes from here another book we shall see. I'm not rushing into anything, I am going to take things slow this time.

      I want to thank everyone for their love and support without y'all this wouldn't be possible. After almost losing my life to someone I did nothing but care about. It made me more cautious when it comes to any type of relationship. I don't tolerate being misused or mistreated, as soon as I see that, I would walk away. I know my worth so I'm no longer settling just because the person is there or I am lonely. I need more than that, will you be there when I am down, angry and lost. When things from my past come to haunt me will you be there to comfort me and let me know everything is going to be ok. Even if it's not, I know what I want out of life now and that's to help people that have been abused, physically and verbally. It hurts and it could break you down. It can make you have insecurities about yourself that you never had before. When you see me post myself having a good time it's because I deserve it. I put myself through too much so now it's time to take care of me, love me and cater to myself. I don't post everything I do all the time because if I did people would say I'm doing too much, I don't think I'm doing enough. When you finally start living life for yourself you can enjoy it. So if you're in a rough situation you don't have to stay there, there is a way out you just have to see it and believe it. I did, it wasn't easy but it was what was best for me. I have a fresh start. I am loving it. Well stay tuned, I'm sure I have another book left in me. Love yous!!